ANNA CLYNE

FITS + STARTS

for Amplified Cello and Tape

Playing Score and Pre-recorded Audio

Electronic files for the pre-recorded tape part are
available from the Boosey & Hawkes Rental Library at
usrental@boosey.com.

BOOSEY & HAWKES

Commissioned by Hysterica Dance Company

First recorded by Benjamin Capps (solo cello)
and Anna Clyne (backing cello and tape)
on "Blue Moth" Tzadik 8084

PERFORMANCE NOTES

This work requires playback of a stereo prerecorded track as well as amplification.

Performances will need 2 high-frequency response stereo speakers, positioned mid-stage far-left and far-right; a subwoofer positioned center stage; a two-channel playback device with stereo output for the tape.

Reverb is to be added to the live cello signal, but not to the prerecorded audio.

A mixer with at least 3 inputs is needed for performance.

Input 1 – cello with reverb (preferably chamber reverb)
Input 2 – left channel of stereo tape (panned hard left)
Input 3 – right channel of stereo tape (panned hard right)

Electronic files for the pre-recorded tape part are available from the Boosey & Hawkes Rental Library at **usrental@boosey.com**.

Commissioned by Hysterica Dance Company

FITS + STARTS

ANNA CLYNE
(2003)

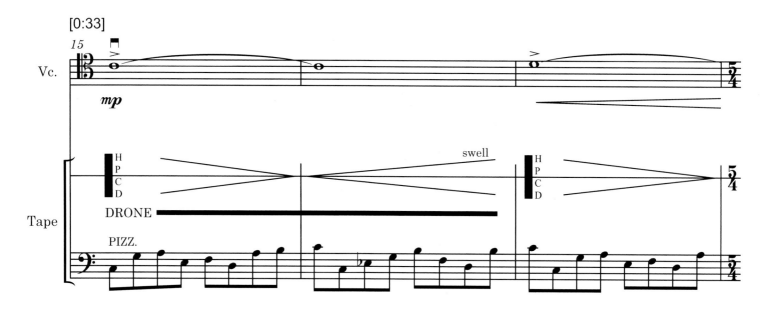

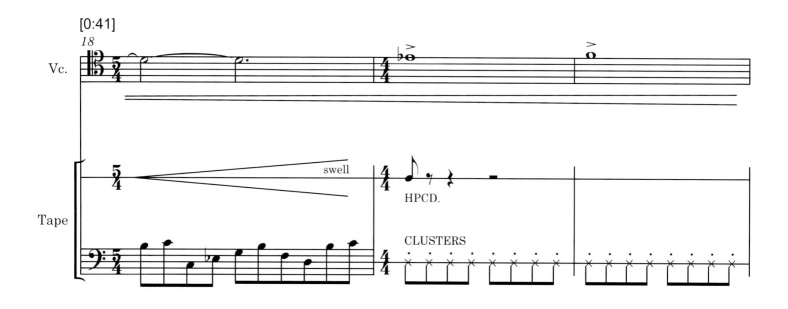

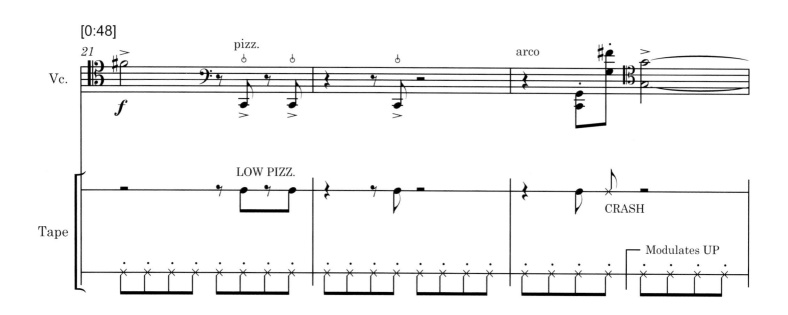

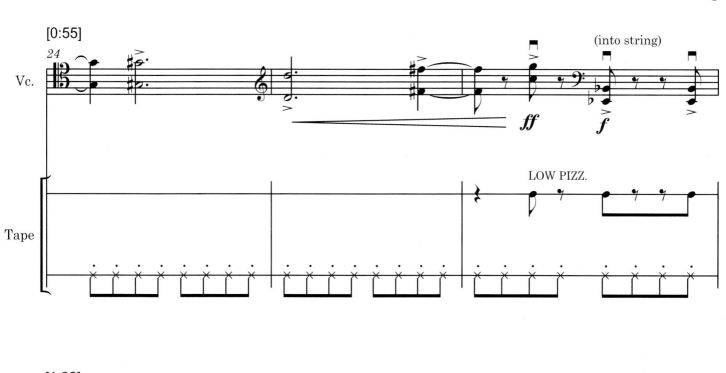

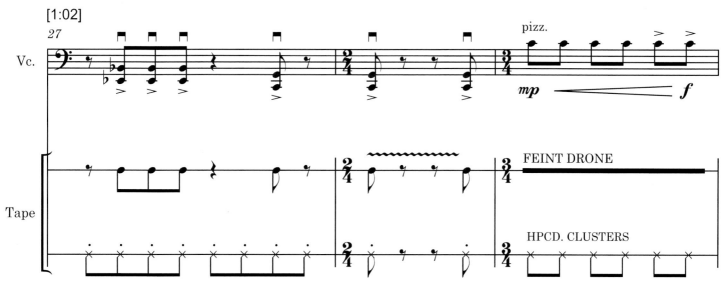

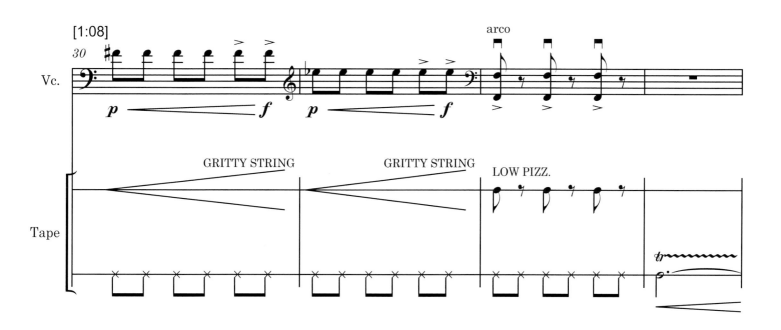

FITS + STARTS

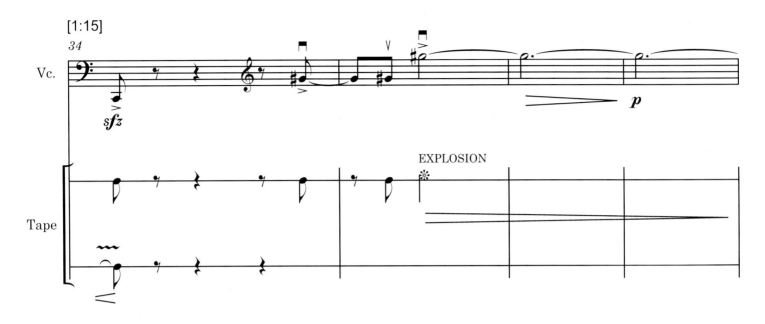

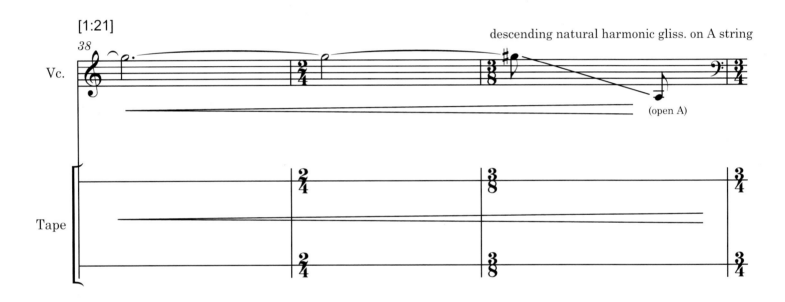

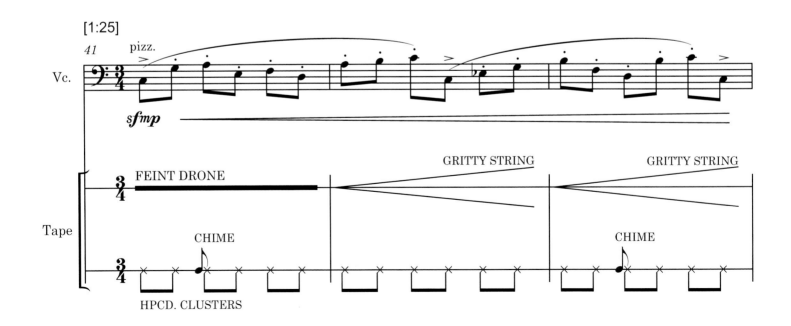

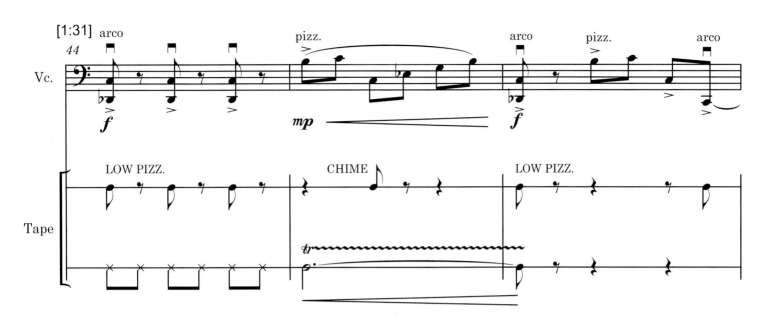

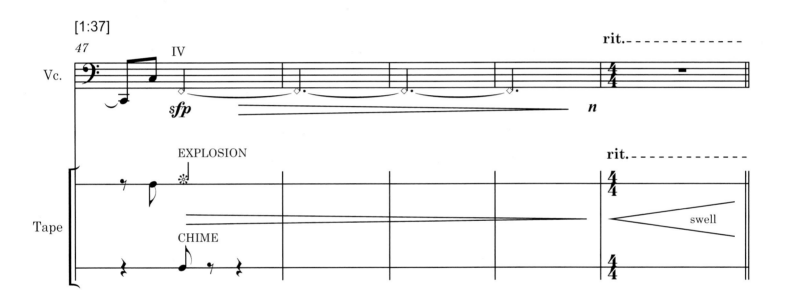

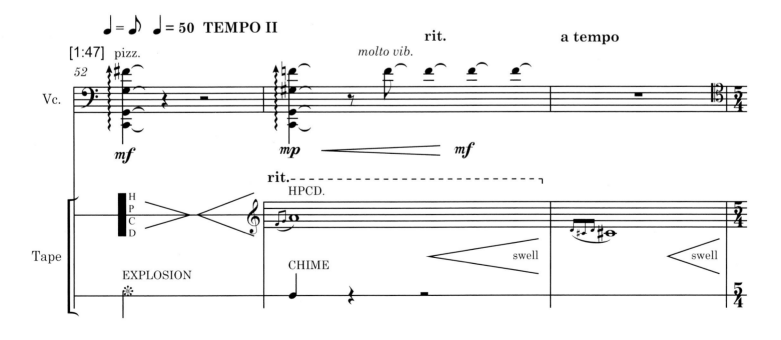

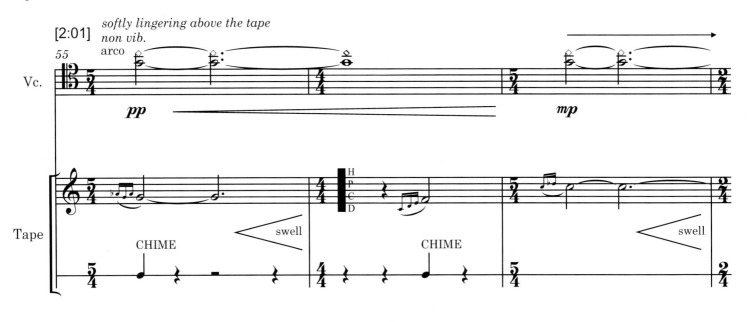

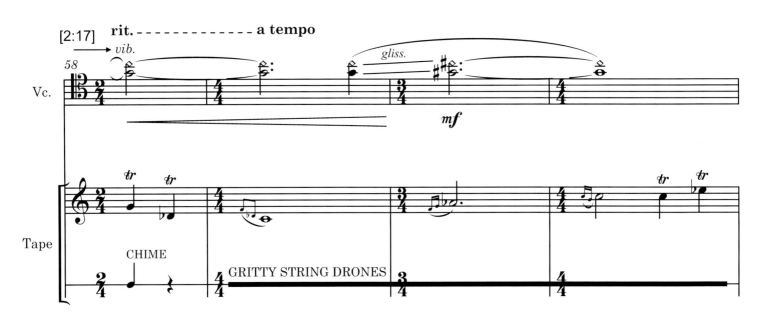

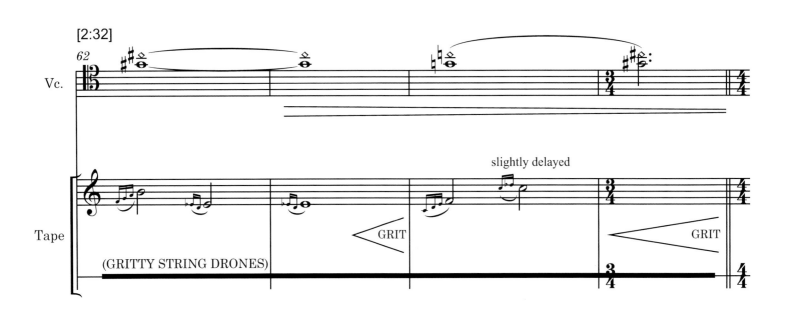

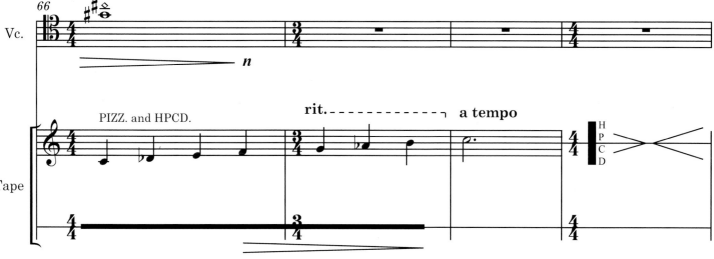

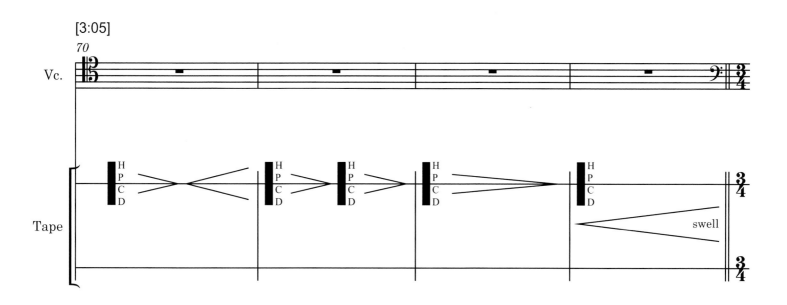

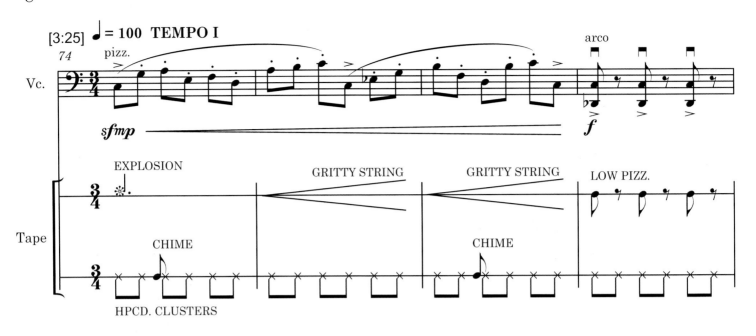

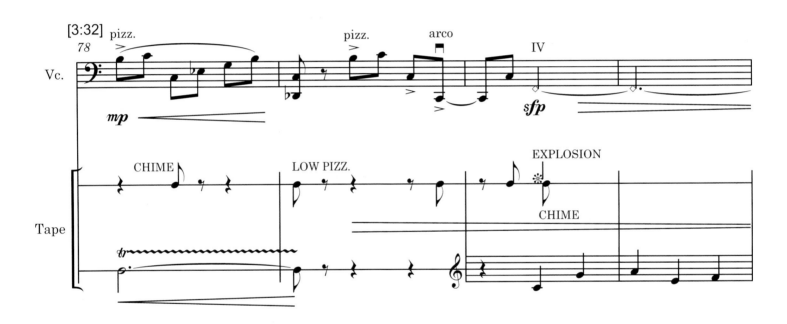

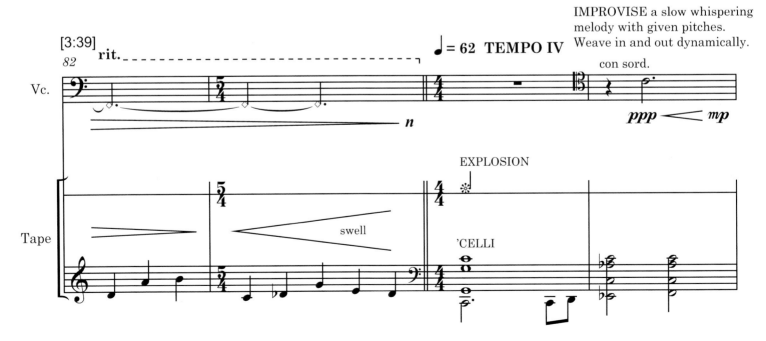

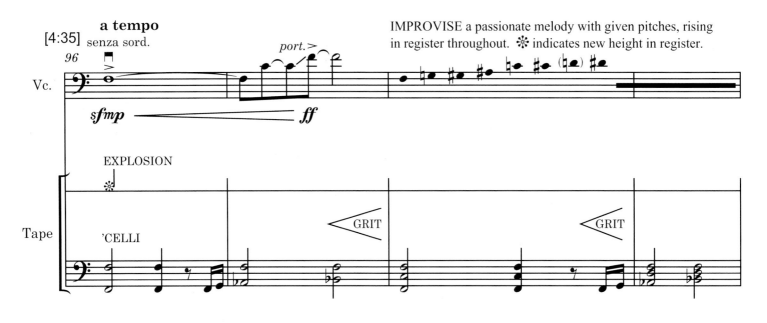

a tempo
[4:35] senza sord.

IMPROVISE a passionate melody with given pitches, rising in register throughout. ✳ indicates new height in register.

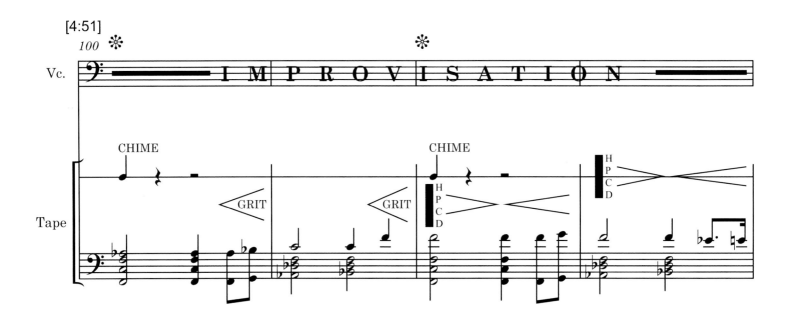

[4:51]

[5:07] Now play in parallel octaves in upper register

Highest notes possible through to end of improvisation

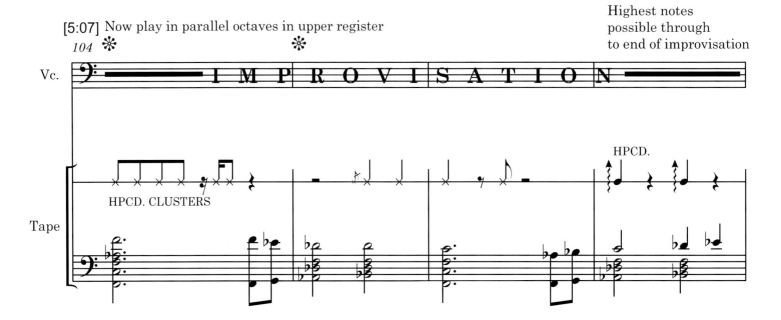

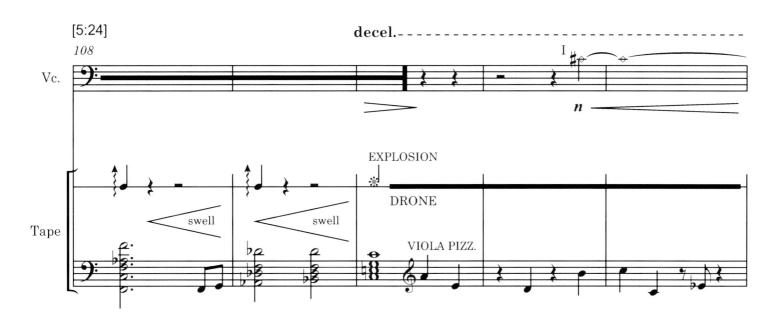

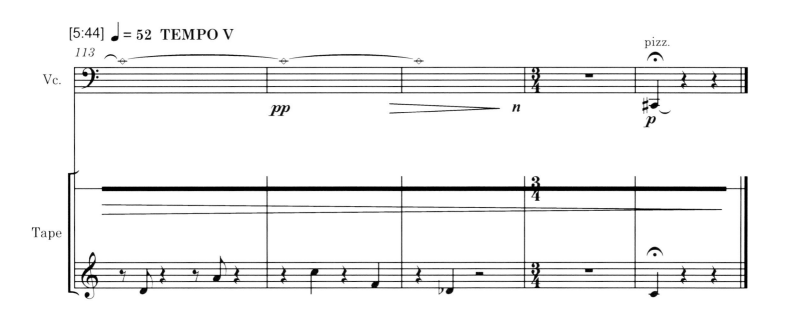